First US edition 2021
First published by Big Picture Press,
an imprint of Bonnier Books UK, 2020

Library of Congress Catalog Card Number pending
ISBN 978-1-5362-1707-0

21 22 23 24 25 26 TLF 10 9 8 7 6 5 4 3 2 1

Printed in Dongguan, Guangdong, China

To Nathalie and Lydia —BT
For Edmund Johnson, with love and thanks —CB

This book was typeset in
Core Circus Rough and Neutraface Text.
The illustrations were created digitally.

BIG PICTURE PRESS
an imprint of
Candlewick Press
99 Dover Street
Somerville, Massachusetts 02144

www.candlewick.com

REPTILES

EVERYWHERE

ILLUSTRATED BY BRITTA TECKENTRUP
WRITTEN BY CAMILLA DE LA BEDOYERE

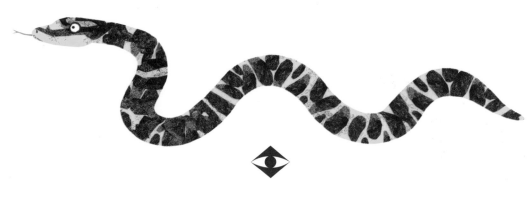

BPP

THERE ARE REPTILES EVERYWHERE

Reptiles are scaly-skinned animals that live in all sorts of places, from salty seas to steamy jungles. There they swim, crawl, run, slither, or glide as they search for food and try to stay out of trouble. The smallest reptiles are no bigger than a thumbnail, while the largest living reptiles can grow to more than 30 feet/9 meters long.

Ankylosaur

Desert tortoise

Blue iguana

Veiled chameleon

Marine iguana

Madagascar giant day gecko

Gila monster

Red-eared terrapin

Pteranodon

Spectacled caiman

Asian forest tortoise

Asian water monitor

Nile crocodile

Green crested lizard

Black-headed bushmaster

Brookesia micra

All these reptiles are out and about in the world today, except two, which are extinct, having died out around 65 to 70 million years ago. Can you spot them?

IT'S A REPTILE!
(SO WHAT *IS* THAT?)

Reptiles don't have fur or feathers. Instead, their skin is covered in scales or bony plates, or both. Most reptiles lay eggs, but some give birth to their babies, as mammals do.

TURTLES AND TORTOISES

Instead of teeth, turtles and tortoises have a hard beak. A tough, bony shell covered in plates, called **scutes**, protects their soft bodies. The top of the shell is called the **carapace**, and the flat bottom is the **plastron**.

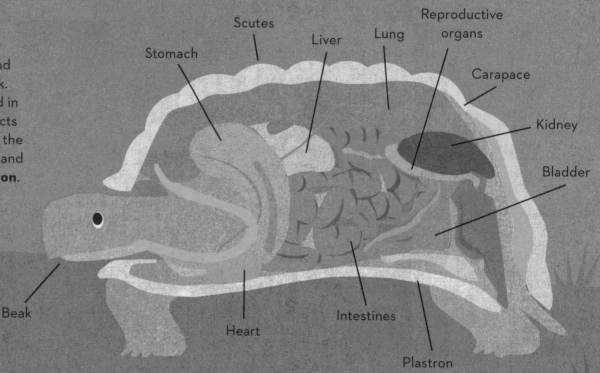

Scutes

Stomach

Liver

Lung

Reproductive organs

Carapace

Kidney

Bladder

Beak

Heart

Intestines

Plastron

COLD BLOOD

Reptiles are cold-blooded. This means that they can't keep their bodies at a steady temperature, as humans and other mammals do. Instead, they have to bask in the sun to warm up. When they get too hot, they have to move into the shade to cool down again.

LUNG POWER

The lungs of marine turtles are a bit like balloons. When their lungs are full of air, the turtles can swim near the surface of the sea.

IT'S A BIG FAMILY!

Did you spot the extinct reptiles, the ankylosaur and pteranodon?

Ankylosaurs were dinosaurs—reptiles that appeared around 240 million years ago and ruled the planet for the next 174 million years.

Pteranodons were huge flying reptiles with long, toothless jaws. They belonged to a group of reptiles called pterosaurs.

CROCODILIANS

There are twenty-five species of crocodilians, large reptiles in the crocodile family. They have long bodies covered in bony scales and long jaws, which they use for snapping up fish. This family includes crocodiles, alligators, caimans, and the endangered gharial, which has a skinny snout lined with sharp teeth.

Gharial

LIZARDS

Lizards have four legs and a tail, and most are speedy movers. Many lizards have sharp claws, but geckos have sticky toes that grip onto branches. Some geckos also have skin flaps that they use to glide briefly through the air.

Kuhl's flying gecko

SNAKES

Snakes are uniquely suited for slithering and sliding. The scales on their underside grip the ground like the sole of a shoe, so they can push themselves forward with their muscles. These muscles move in waves, making the body move from side to side in an S shape.

Vertebrae

Stomach

Liver

Large intestine

Kidneys

Reproductive organs

Small intestine

Trachea

Fangs

Forked tongue

Ribs

Lung

Heart

Crocodilians are the closest living relatives to dinosaurs. Like the ankylosaur, they have bony plates on their bodies.

You can still see dinosaur-like features in modern reptiles. Male **Jackson's chameleons** have three horns, which make them look a bit like a **triceratops**!

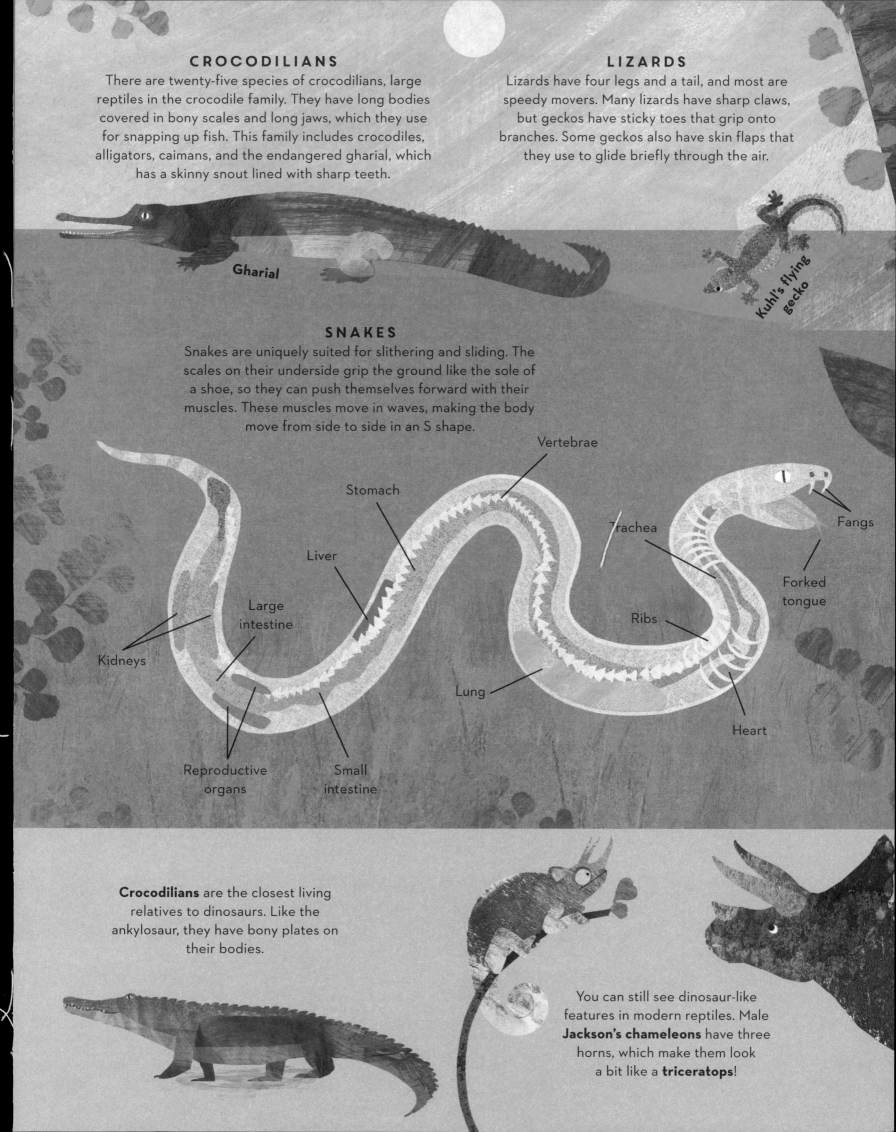

REPTILES HAVE BEEN AROUND FOR AGES

Reptiles have been around for 312 million years, long before furry or feathered animals appeared. To put this into perspective, modern humans have been on the planet for only about 200,000 years!

Tetrapodophis was a strange-looking snake with four tiny legs that lived 120 million years ago. It used its long body to squeeze its prey to death, just as modern constrictor snakes do.

Tetrapodophis

340–330 MILLION YEARS AGO

Balanerpeton

Protosuchus

The first crocodilians, such as *Protosuchus*, looked like long-legged lizards and were probably fast movers both on land and in the water. They had strong jaws and hunted their prey alongside dinosaurs.

All reptiles evolved from a group of animals called amphibians. *Balanerpeton* was an early amphibian; it laid its eggs in water, just as modern frogs and toads do.

Eunotosaurus

Hylonomus

Eunotosaurus is the earliest known member of the turtle family. It had large, wide ribs that may have been the evolutionary beginnings of a turtle shell.

Hylonomus was probably one of the first reptiles to evolve, about 312 million years ago. It had sharp teeth, which it used for eating bugs, and it laid its eggs on land.

By 210 million years ago, there were reptiles with bony shells, but **Proganochelys** looked much scarier than modern turtles. It had rows of spikes around its neck and a spiky tail that ended in a club—useful for walloping any predators that wanted to eat it.

Proganochelys

Sarcosuchus

Sarcosuchus was a mighty meat-eating monster as long as a bus. This mega-croc had giant jaws lined with more than 120 teeth. It lived 112 million years ago.

Archelon

Archelon, the largest turtle ever, lived in oceans 70 million years ago and hunted soft, squishy jellyfish, squid, and octopuses. It grew to 13 feet/4 meters long—that's the length of an elephant!

TODAY

A **tuatara** looks like a lizard, but it's not. It's a reptile that's been called a living fossil because it is so similar to reptiles that lived at the time of the dinosaurs. The tuatara and its ancestors have been in New Zealand for more than 80 million years.

Tuatara

Amazingly, some reptiles did survive. Six million years after the asteroid crashed into Earth, enormous snakes like **Titanoboa**— more than 46 feet/14 meters long—were slithering through steamy prehistoric rain forests.

Titanoboa

Around 66 million years ago, an enormous ball of burning rock came from space and slammed into Earth. It caused huge fires, and clouds of deadly smoke filled the sky. Three-quarters of all animals and plants went extinct.

WHERE DO REPTILES LIVE?

Reptiles prefer warm places, but they can make their homes almost anywhere. All they need is something to eat, somewhere to warm up, and shelter when they need to rest, hide, or cool down.

CUNNING CAVE SNAKES

A dark and gloomy cave is not the ideal hunting ground for most reptiles, but a cave in Kantemó, Mexico, serves up a delicious meal for **yellow-red rat snakes**. As the sun rises, they simply hang upside down from the cave ceiling and wait for supper to arrive. At dawn, hundreds of bats return to the cave to sleep—only to be gobbled up by these ravenous suspended snakes.

Yelllow-red rat snake

Marine iguana

SALTY SEA SNAKES

The **yellow-bellied sea snake** spends its whole life at sea, using its flat, paddle-shaped tail to swim. When it finds a tasty fish, it swims backward to get its fangs in the perfect position, then strikes with its deadly venom.

Yellow-bellied sea snake

DEEP-SEA DIVERS

Marine iguanas live on the Galápagos Islands, off the coast of Ecuador, and take a daily plunge into the Pacific Ocean. They hold their breath for over half an hour while they swim to the seabed and nibble on seaweed.

CHILLY LIZARDS

On New Zealand's Stewart Island, the weather can turn wet and windy in the winter. **Harlequin geckos** have a clever way of coping with the cold. Their usually bright skin turns dark, enabling them to soak up sunlight faster.

Harlequin gecko

DESERT REPTILES

Reptiles rule in hot, dry deserts, where it rarely rains and few plants can grow. Snakes and lizards bask in the strong desert sun, which quickly warms up their muscles so they can chase bugs and scorpions.

SIDEWINDERS

Most snakes struggle to move across deserts. All those tiny grains of sand keep moving, making it difficult to grip onto the ground. **Mexican desert sidewinders** scoot across the slippery sand by throwing their bodies into S-shaped coils. Only two parts of their body touch the hot sand at a time, so it's a cool way to travel—and speedy, too.

COOLING DOWN

The Sonoran Desert, in North America, is baking hot in the day but becomes very nippy at night. **Desert tortoises** dig burrows, giving themselves somewhere to hide from the sun during the day and stay snug at night. Their feet are shovel-shaped, so they're perfect for digging through soft sand.

Mexican desert sidewinder

Desert tortoise

ANT EATERS

Spiky-skinned **thorny devils** live in Australia's Great Sandy Desert. They lap up passing ants with their sticky tongues, gobbling up hundreds at a time.

A spiny body is handy when it's time for a drink. Overnight, the desert cools down and dew collects on the lizard's back. The water runs along little grooves between its spikes and pours into its mouth.

Thorny devil

RAIN FOREST REPTILES

Borneo, a large island in Southeast Asia, is a reptile's paradise. From the longest snake in the world to a flying dragon, more than 250 species of reptiles thrive in the steamy heat of the island's rain forest. It's nice and warm, and there's plenty of food as well as lots of places to hide.

Asian forest tortoise

Draco lizard

Watch out—this **Draco lizard** is on the move! Thin sheets of skin between its ribs act like a parachute as it glides from tree to tree. Gliding is much faster than climbing up and down.

The **Asian forest tortoise** protects her eggs by piling a mound of leaves over them. If a predator comes snooping around, she adds more leaves and stands on top of the mound.

Spiny terrapins keep their guard up. They may have a hard, sharp-edged shell, but that's no defense against fierce neighborhood predators like the saltwater crocodile.

Spiny terrapin

A **saltwater crocodile** lurks in the shadows. Its nostrils and eyes are on top of its head, so it can stay out of view while watching for something tasty— like a nice, crunchy spiny terrapin—to cruise by.

Saltwater crocodile

CAN YOU FIND IT?
Small and dainty, the **green crested lizard** scuttles through the trees. Its bright-green skin blends in with the background, but it turns brown when it's scared. There are six green crested lizards hiding in this scene. How many of them are feeling frightened?

Tokay gecko

Beware a hungry **blue coral snake**! Its bright-orange head and tail are a warning that it's very dangerous, with venom that can kill in minutes. Luckily, its favorite food isn't people but other deadly snakes!

A strange sound can be heard in the rainforest. It's a colorful **tokay gecko**, named after the male's loud call of "to-kay, to-kay," made to attract a mate.

Blue coral snake

Anyone brave enough to put their head inside a **false gharial**'s mouth would be able to count more than 80 razor-sharp, pointy teeth.

False gharial

The **sailfin** has a miraculous talent. When it takes fright, it heads to the river and runs across the water. It doesn't sink right away because it runs so quickly and has big, wide feet that trap air beneath them.

Reticulated python

Sailfin lizard

The world's longest snake is about to take a dip. It's a **reticulated python**, and it can grow to a monstrous 33 feet/10 meters long. Female pythons lay their eggs in hollow trees and stay with them until they hatch.

FEEDING

Of the thousands of reptiles around the world, some eat plants, some eat other animals, and some eat both!

MEET THE HERBIVORES

On the tropical island of Madagascar foliage abounds!

SWEET TOOTH
At night, **geckos** set out to find food. Some of them hunt bugs, but others prefer the sugary liquid that flowers make, called nectar.

Radiated tortoise

Peacock day gecko

SLOW AND STEADY
Turtles and **tortoises** are slow-moving creatures, so they can't chase and catch fast-moving animals. Instead, most of them munch on plants or on little bugs that they can snap up in their beak-like mouths.

Madagascar day gecko

CAN YOU FIND IT?
Brookesia **chameleons** hide from predators by pretending to be dead leaves, which is easy when you are brown, scaly, and smaller than a thumb. How many can you count on this page?

Standing's day gecko

Phelsuma masohoala

MEET THE CARNIVORES

Snakes, crocodilians, and lizards the world over have some of the most impressive hunting skills in the animal kingdom.

Carpet python

SIT AND WAIT

Pythons and **boas** are **ambush predators**, which means they lie around waiting for their prey to wander past. Since their patterned skin blends into the background, their victims never see them coming.

Veiled chameleon

ELASTIC TONGUES

Chameleons have the longest tongue of any lizard—up to one and a half times their body length! It comes in handy for catching bugs that think they're safely out of reach. The chameleon's super-speedy sticky tongue shoots out like a slingshot—zap, crunch, and gulp!

SPECIAL SENSES

We use our eyes and nose to see and smell food, but **pit vipers** have an extra-super sense for tracking down their lunch: special pits beneath their eyes can sense the heat coming off other animals' bodies.

White-lipped pit viper

Nile crocodile

A DEADLY DIVE

The **death roll** is the secret weapon of all crocodilians and a nasty way to go! Using their strong jaws, they drag their prey underwater to drown them, then spin around to tear the body apart.

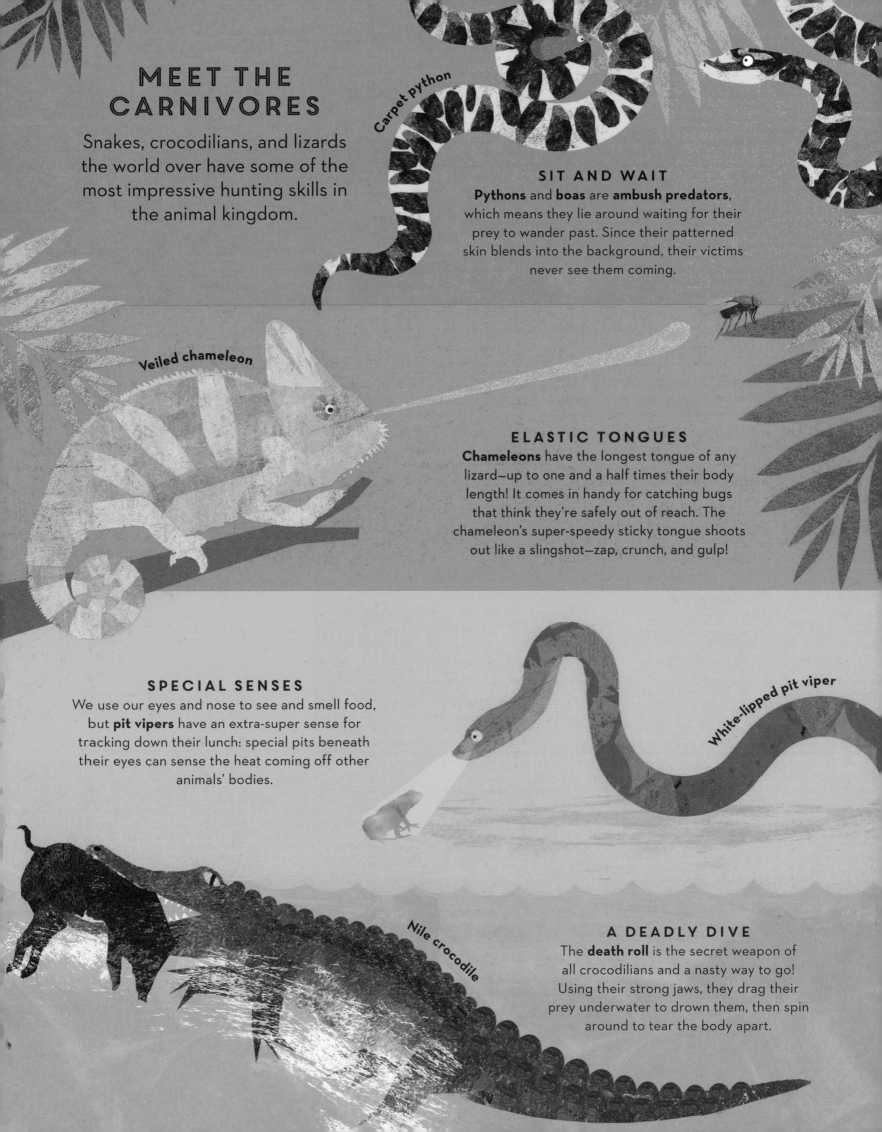

KOMODO DRAGONS

Growing up to 10 feet/3 meters long, the biggest lizard in the world is the mighty **Komodo dragon**. These ferocious predators live only on Komodo Island, in Indonesia, and on other small islands nearby. They can swallow a goat whole and will later throw up everything they can't digest—leaving a stinking pile of teeth, fur, horns, and hooves.

DRAGON WEAPONS

Komodo dragons have killer instincts and scary weapons to match their size and strength. They can run at top speeds of 12 miles/20 kilometers an hour, but Komodo dragons rarely use their speed to hunt—they prefer to ambush their prey instead.

Teeth and **saliva:** A Komodo dragon has nearly sixty teeth, serrated like a bread knife for maximum damage. They also have venomous saliva, which enters their victim's bloodstream once it's been bitten.

CAN YOU FIND IT?
Hungry Komodo dragons sometimes munch on tender, juicy *baby* Komodo dragons! Can you spot a baby dragon hiding from the grown-ups?

Muscles: Strong, sturdy legs and a powerful tail are useful weapons for scrapping with other Komodo dragons.

MEET THE FAMILY

Komodo dragons belong to a group of reptiles called **monitor lizards**. Monitor lizards, Mexican beaded lizards, and Gila monsters are all part of the same family, a group of lizards called **anguimorphs**.

MEGALANIA

How would you feel about having a 16-foot/5-meter-long lizard as a neighbor? Forty thousand years ago, giant lizards called *Megalania* lived alongside people in Australia. They were almost twice the size of Komodo dragons.

GILA MONSTER

Despite their scary name, **Gila monsters** use their venomous bite only to defend themselves, and their bright stripes warn predators to stay away—so not that scary, really. These lizards grow up to 20 inches/50 centimeters long.

MEXICAN BEADED LIZARD

The **Mexican beaded lizard** is highly venomous, but it's also very shy and is usually hidden away in its forest burrow. These lizards store fat in their oversize tail as an energy reserve. The lizards can grow to nearly 3 feet/1 meter long, but almost half of that is tail!

THE ATTACK

Komodo dragons don't mind waiting for dinner, because they can survive for days without eating. They spend hours on a forest track, hiding in the shadows while they wait for a pig or deer to come by . . . then they pounce.

Senses: Komodo dragons can't see or hear very well, but they have a great sense of taste and smell thanks to their forked tongue.

Jaws: Strong jaws are good for crushing crunchy bones. A Komodo dragon can open its jaws very wide, which makes it easier to wolf down big chunks of food.

Claws: These can grow to 2 inches/5 centimeters long and are sharp and curved, perfect for plunging into prey.

THE END

Brute strength allows Komodo dragons to overpower their prey in seconds. Even if a pig, goat, or deer manages to escape the predator's deadly grip, it will soon die from the effects of its venom. Komodo dragons can devour up to 80 percent of their own body weight in a single meal.

SUNSHINE, SHADE, AND SLEEP

Reptiles' bodies work a bit differently from ours. They need to warm up their blood and muscles by lying in the sunshine, known as **basking**. But if they get too hot, they have to slip into the shade to cool down. That's why they are often on the move, scurrying from sunshine to shade, trying to control their body temperature. In the winter, reptiles in very cold parts of the world go into a period of inactivity called **brumation**.

TEMPERATURE CONTROL

Human bodies stay at a steady temperature of 98.6°F/37°C. We control our temperature by making heat inside our bodies when we get too cold and by sweating to cool down if we are too hot. This makes us **warm-blooded animals**, just like birds and other mammals.

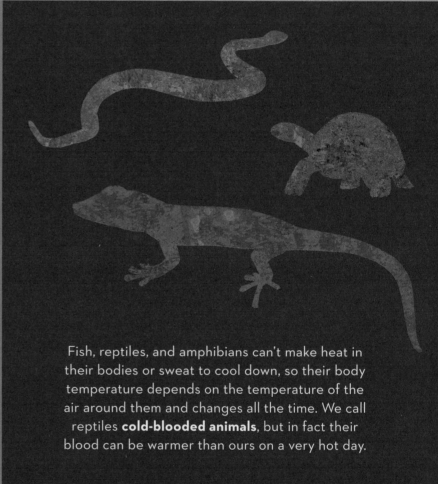

Fish, reptiles, and amphibians can't make heat in their bodies or sweat to cool down, so their body temperature depends on the temperature of the air around them and changes all the time. We call reptiles **cold-blooded animals**, but in fact their blood can be warmer than ours on a very hot day.

BRUMATION

WINTER SLEEPS

Most reptiles live alone, but in cold weather it's a good idea to huddle together for warmth. **European lizards** survive long, cold winters by finding a safe place to snooze through the coldest months. They don't have to eat, but they may wake up a few times if they get thirsty and need a drink.

European lizards

TO WARM UP . . .

a reptile basks in the sunshine. It needs to be able to move quickly if it wants to hunt or escape from danger, but it can only do this once its blood and muscles are warm enough. Sunbathing reptiles have to be careful of sunstroke, though—if they get too hot, they have to find somewhere cooler to bring their body temperature down.

Rainbow agama

TO COOL DOWN . . .

a reptile seeks shade. If it gets too cold, though, its muscles won't work very well and it will have to rest rather than go looking for food.

Luckily, reptiles don't use as much energy as warm-blooded animals, so most of them will happily go for days without eating.

Copperhead snakes

WASTE NOT, WANT NOT

During brumation, the digestive system of some reptiles, like the **marginated tortoise**, slows way down. There's no point producing energy that's not going to be used.

Marginated tortoise

SNAKE SLUMBER PARTY

When autumn comes, **copperhead snakes** return to their dens, which are usually hollow logs or spaces between rocks. Many of them huddle together, sharing their body warmth to keep winter chills away.

STAYING ALIVE

From the moment a reptile pokes it head out into the world, it has to be quick on its feet. There are hungry hunters everywhere, looking for an opportunity to grab a scaly snack. Luckily, reptiles have lots of clever ways of staying alive.

HIDE!
The colors and patterns of reptiles' skin—in stripes, spots, blotches, and speckles—provide effective **camouflage**, enabling them to blend into their surroundings.

CAN YOU FIND IT?
There are fifteen species of **leaf-tailed geckos** in Madagascar. The color and texture of their skin are a perfect match for their lush rain forest surroundings. How many are hiding here?

Milk snake

South American coral snake

MASTERS OF SURVIVAL

LOOK SCARY—EVEN IF YOU'RE NOT!

Milk snakes are harmless, but their colors fool predators into thinking they're as dangerous as a coral snake.

LOOK SCARY!

Bright colors sometimes work as a warning sign. The red, black, and yellow stripes on a **South American coral snake** tell predators to go away.

BE PRICKLY!

Armadillo lizards are covered in spiny scales. If they are attacked, they grab their tail in their mouth and curl into a prickly ball to protect themselves.

Armadillo lizard

LOOK SICKLY!

A **Texas horned lizard** makes itself look too gross to eat by squirting blood from its eyes. It's only 5 inches/13 centimeters long, but predators steer clear of this tiny terror after such a shocking display.

Texas horned lizard

LOOK BIG!

When a **frilled lizard** is frightened, it opens its mouth wide and raises its huge neck frill. If looking big and scary doesn't work, it turns tail and runs for its life.

Frilled lizard

TAKE COVER!

Turtles and **tortoises** use their strong bony shells to stay safe. They pull their head and legs inside and wait for danger to pass.

Greek tortoise

BE DEADLY!

Many snakes are equipped with one of the best defenses in the animal kingdom: venom. It's made in poison glands that are attached to the snake's teeth. Some snakes even inject venom with special hollow fangs.

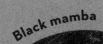

Black mamba

SOUND SCARY!

When a **rattlesnake** hisses, it's a warning to keep a safe distance. To make even more of a racket, it shakes the rattle (made of dead skin) on the tip of its tail. Smart animals hear the warning and move off, fast.

Mojave rattlesnake

REPTILE PARENTS

Unlike mammals, which give birth to live young, most reptiles lay eggs. The females of many species then leave their offspring to fend for themselves, but others take the job of parenting more seriously. Before they start a family, though, reptiles have to find a way to attract a mate.

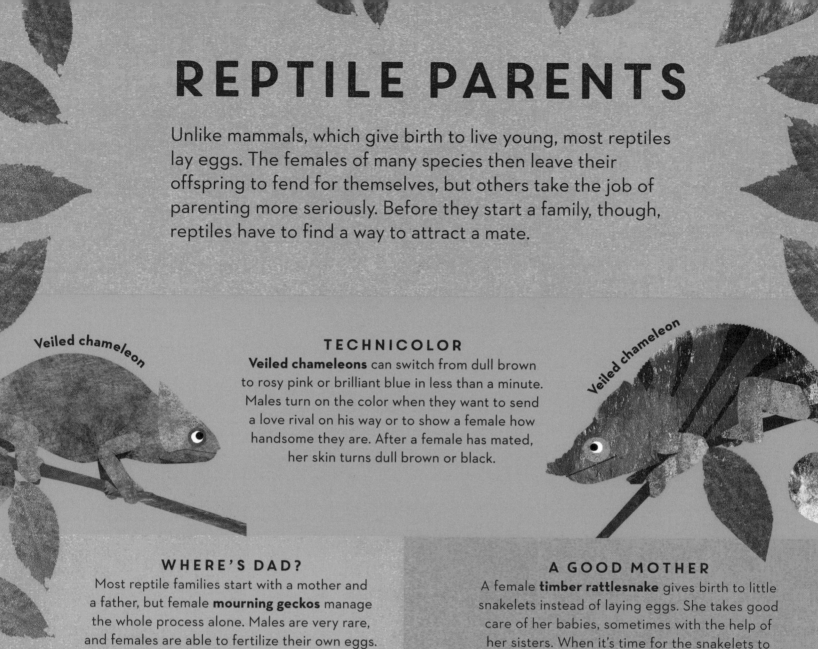

Veiled chameleon

Veiled chameleon

TECHNICOLOR

Veiled chameleons can switch from dull brown to rosy pink or brilliant blue in less than a minute. Males turn on the color when they want to send a love rival on his way or to show a female how handsome they are. After a female has mated, her skin turns dull brown or black.

WHERE'S DAD?

Most reptile families start with a mother and a father, but female **mourning geckos** manage the whole process alone. Males are very rare, and females are able to fertilize their own eggs.

A GOOD MOTHER

A female **timber rattlesnake** gives birth to little snakelets instead of laying eggs. She takes good care of her babies, sometimes with the help of her sisters. When it's time for the snakelets to live alone, their mother shows them the best spots to make a den.

Mourning gecko

Timber rattlesnake

TOO HOT FOR BOYS

Alligator snapping turtles spend most of their lives in lakes or rivers, but in the summer, females bury up to fifty eggs in a sandy riverbank. If the summer is hot, most of the hatchlings will be females. If the weather is cooler, most of the eggs will be males.

Alligator snapping turtles

PARENTING SKILLS: NILE CROCODILES

1. It's mating time, and adult **Nile crocodiles** gather by lakes and rivers. To attract a female, the males swish their tail around in the water and blow bubbles. If a female enjoys the show, she joins the male in the water. The couple swims together in a watery dance before they mate.

2. Once she's ready to lay her eggs, the female digs a hole in the riverbank. She lays up to sixty eggs in the hole, then gently covers them with soil and grass to hide them from hungry predators.

3. For the next three months, the mother stays with the nest night and day, lying on top and fighting off attackers if she needs to. She won't even leave to eat.

4. When the eggs are ready to hatch, the baby crocodiles call their mother from inside their shells. She hears their loud "umph umph" calls and starts to dig the eggs out of the nest.

5. Fathers sometimes help the hatchlings by gently rolling the eggs in their mouth until they break open.

6. The mother takes the baby crocs down to the river, carrying each one tenderly in her giant jaws.

7. The proud croc parents protect the hatchlings in the water, fending off crabs, fish, birds, and mongooses. They look after their babies until they are big enough to live alone.

A TURTLE'S TRAVELS

As the sun sets on a tropical beach, a pile of sand begins to move. Buried deep beneath the surface, a tiny **leatherback turtle** is hatching. She is about to start an epic journey across the Pacific Ocean.

The moon appears above the shores of Papua New Guinea. The moon's silvery light is reflected on the water and will guide this young female and her many siblings—up to one hundred hatchlings in total—from their sandy nest toward the sea.

The baby turtle swims down to the seabed, where the water drags her out to the open ocean. She feeds on little plants and animals while the water pulls her farther and farther out to sea.

The waves sweep her up and carry her into deeper water, where fish gather in the hope of catching a snack. She is small enough to fit inside a teacup, so this is a dangerous time.

Leatherback turtles return to the beaches where they hatched to lay their own eggs. They probably use the Earth's magnetic field to find their way, but exactly how they do this is a mystery!

The little turtle starts swimming across the Pacific Ocean and, after a few years, reaches shallow seas on the other side of the ocean, along the Pacific coast of North America. There's plenty of food here, so she eats well and grows until she is 7 feet/2 meters long. At this great size, she is too big for most predators to attack her.

Once she reaches the beach, the turtle will lay her eggs, carefully burying them in the sand. Then she will shuffle back into the water and head east, ready for a long journey back to the other side of the world.

Now it's time to head west, back to the beach in New Guinea where the turtle began her life. It takes her more than a year to travel across the Pacific Ocean. She swims an incredible 10,000 miles/16,000 kilometers.

CAN YOU FIND IT?
In their early years, young turtles are in great danger of being eaten by birds, crabs, squid, and fish, including sharks. Can you spot some predators searching for a snack?

REPTILES AND PEOPLE

There is a long history between reptiles and humans. In the past we have worshipped reptiles, often we fear them, and scientists have spent a lot of time studying them to find out more about the Earth and how it has changed over time. More recently, people are trying to find ways to live in harmony with reptiles, learning more about how we can protect them and their homes for years to come.

MYTHS AND LEGENDS

All around the world, people have honored reptiles in religion and mythology. Central American cultures featured a feathered snake-god called **Quetzalcoatl**, worshipped as the creator of the world and the god of winds and rain.

DINOSAUR FEVER

Everyone is fascinated by the most famous reptiles of them all: **dinosaurs.** Fossils of about fifty new dinosaur species are discovered every year. Scientists study them to learn more about how reptiles have evolved over time.

DEADLY REPTILES

Most reptiles aren't dangerous, but in some parts of the world humans have a good reason to fear them. Australia has more venomous snakes than any other country. Just a few drops of poison from an **inland taipan** could kill one hundred humans.

REPTILES AND TECHNOLOGY

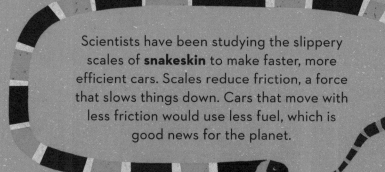

Chameleons can change the color of their skin. This skill could be used to make clothes that change color in a flash! Scientists have already worked out how to make some fabrics change color when the temperature changes.

Scientists have been studying the slippery scales of **snakeskin** to make faster, more efficient cars. Scales reduce friction, a force that slows things down. Cars that move with less friction would use less fuel, which is good news for the planet.

REPTILES AT RISK

Reptiles may not be very cute or fluffy, but they play an important role in our world. All over the planet, people are working hard to help reptiles survive and thrive. This type of work is called **conservation**.

CITIZEN SCIENCE

In citizen science projects, groups of volunteers explore a local area to find and count different types of reptiles. This helps scientists learn more about reptiles and find ways to protect them.

VOLUNTEER

In warm coastal places like Kefalonia, Greece, volunteers and scientists work together to protect sea turtle eggs as they hatch and guide the baby turtles to the sea.

BOUNCING BACK

Thanks to conservation, some reptiles that were once nearly extinct are now thriving. Not so long ago, there were fewer than twenty-five **blue iguanas** in the wild. Now there may be nearly a thousand! They live in the Cayman Islands, in the Caribbean Sea.

A CHANGING WORLD

Reptiles are great survivors, but now they face some big challenges. If we help protect them and their ecosystems—both at home and far away—they could still have a bright future.

For more than 2,000 years, doctors have used the **venom** of some reptiles to develop **medicines** that treat snakebites. Today, reptile venom helps make medicines to treat diabetes and blood diseases.

Scientists have been studying **geckos' sticky feet**, hoping to find ideas about how to make new kinds of glue, as well as robots that can climb up the sides of buildings, repair bridges, or even clean satellites in space.